It's Not Your Fault

Gia Menon

BookLeaf
Publishing

India | USA | UK

Presentation by *BookLeaf Publishing*

Web: www.bookleafpub.com

E-mail: info@bookleafpub.com

ISBN: 9789357447225

First edition 2022

Dedicated to my family and friends, my rock in this uncertain world. You know who you are.

ACKNOWLEDGEMENT

Is a journey even worth writing about if it was plain sailing?

I acknowledge my victories and downfalls. To the ones who attempted to break me and to the ones who attempted to heal me. .

To my readers…
You are powerful, you are magic.
Hang in there.

PREFACE

To the unhealed child in you, the raging soul within you and the beauty in the courage you have mustered.

You are not your silent battles and scars; you are the strength in moments you embraced your wounds and watched them heal. Each part of you that once broke, growing bigger and better. Stronger and newer.

This book will not sugarcoat anything for you. These are the things you are longing to tell yourself.

This is for you.

You

Persevere, until the end.

You lie there baring that soul,
looking like poetry
that willingly hides
behind words
Words that the human mind
cannot wrap its head around
Time after time,
reconsidering reality,
questioning existence,
yet blending into
this everyday madness
that surrounds you

Persevere, until the end.

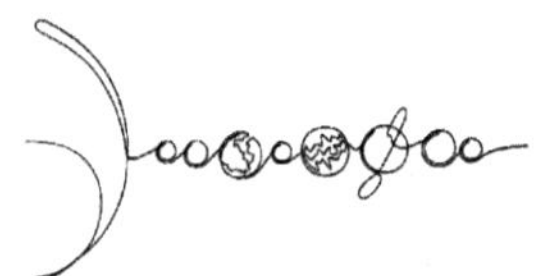

Claim

It is about time.

As vast as the breadth
of your dreams
More magical than the
existence of being

Secrets deeper than the
questions you seek
Maybe it's science,
a world entangled
in cosmic beams

Been there for you
for longer than you
would ever know
Furtively tingling
through every inch
of your bone

Theories and beliefs
don't justify a thing
But what you wish for,
the universe will bring

It is about time.

The Horizon

You are the horizon.

Doubts and uncertainties
may dull your shine
But you are stardust
with dreams floating
in those hopeful eyes

Tread on thin ice
Fall once twice thrice
But, get back up
and
put up a fight

Carry those wounds
not as a reflection
of your pain
But to wrap it around
like an armor
As you walk into the rough sea,
gracefully sinking in valor

You are the horizon.

Emerge

The only way up is to rise.
Lost in dissonance
Trying to find silence
in this deafening noise

Even when you are breaking
There is an indistinct voice
holding on to you with dear life

Pause, not to crumble
but to wonder how you've
conquered pain even in
the absence of your
absolute mind

Gently let the dark side in
Have a conversation with
the trickeries of time

You'll see how you lay
those fears on a stained platter
Finding strength in loving
closed chapters

The only way up is to rise.

Gauge

May you recognize
real love that day.

My father once told me,
you will find the kind who
will tell you they love you,
caress every morsel of you,
and devour you like you are
the only thing they want,
and then leave you feeling
empty

And then,
there will be a kind
who won't talk much about
love, but would choose you
every day in subtle ways

May you recognize
real love that day.

Unashamed

Break down often,
unashamedly.

When you break down,
you break the possibility of
false laughters
You break the possibility of
evading an "I'm okay"
You break the misleading
perception of strength

You break the idea of
strength masked in insecurities
You break the world's
frivolous rose tinted glasses
You break the silence that
that is glorified as power
So please,

Break down often,
unashamedly.

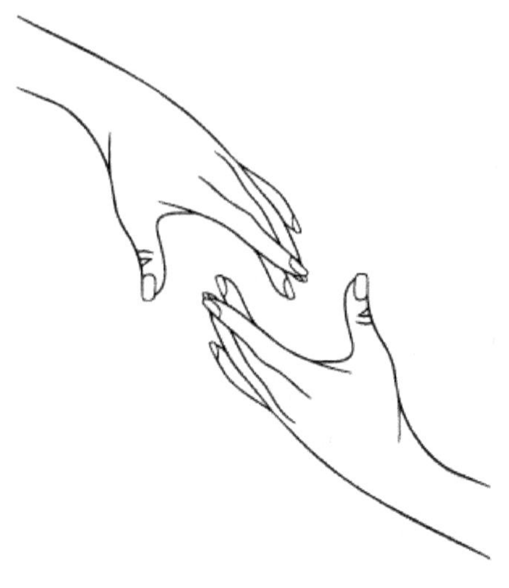

Embrace

Don't trick your mind into
believing everything is alright.

Tell yourself that it hurts,
but you are trying
Toss and turn all night,
but embrace the void
every time you wake up
Show yourself the demons
within, and how you are
willing to fight them one at a time
Walk on the edge of
losing your sanity,
then sit yourself down,
weave stories that fight denial
Accept that you're human,
you failed
only to get familiar with
winning again

Feel your bones crumble within
and then watch yourself heal

Don't trick your mind into
believing everything is alright.

Clarity

When you distance and detach,
you learn.

Not about them, but about you
Of the ways you convinced
your heart it was deserving
of all the careless apologies,
the inconsistent fondness,
and plenty of justified
uncertainties
Nothing less, nothing more,

You learn,
about where exactly
your heart creases when you
smile or let that cry out,
of stories that were locked up
in quaint corners of your heart
Suddenly you learn how sitting
down with yourself at the
corner table in a coffee shop
doesn't mean you are lonely
You see how those long walks
were actually conversations with
your inner child and a mere
initiation for your unspoken healing

When you distance and detach,
you learn

Unbecoming

Real beauty lies in these
moments of brutal unbecoming.

The beauty of letting go
lies not in the day you
wake up feeling free
It lies in the nights
when you cried your
self-doubts to sleep,
when washing away
self-love felt justifiable,
when believing in nothing
seemed easier than
believing in yourself,
but you still gathered
everything you hold
with a hint of hope
You slipped into a dark
place, but refused to
let it consume you,
and chose to re-paint it
against your will

Real beauty lies in these
moments of brutal unbecoming.

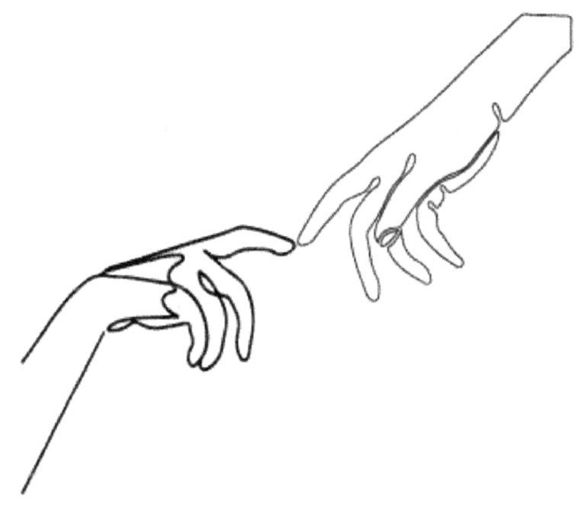

Undo

Stop polluting the idea of beauty
with flesh and bones
at the core of it

Let us make it more about
scars and unsung battles,
birthing new life,
wounds that ended in victory,
disfigurements that boast of courage,
hearts that unconditionally give away,
minds that willingly hold your pain,
every one that wakes up every day
with nothing but hope to live another day

Stop polluting the idea of beauty
with flesh and bones
at the core of it.

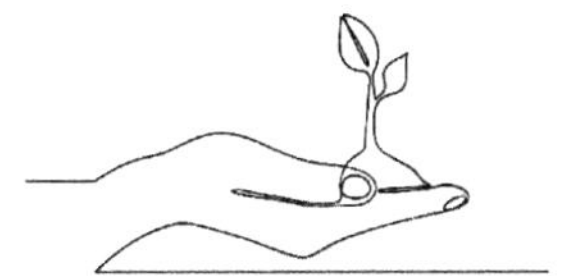

Eternal

You shall forever
carry it with grace.

Touched by hands that
never knew respect,
convinced all this while that
your self-worth has been
diminished to crumbs
Little do you know it is
just the skin and bones
they could take over
Real strength still remains,
lingering in pieces of your soul

And you shall forever
carry it with grace.

Tonight

There's only so much
I can do tonight.

I replay all the years that
passed by in silent grief,
every move weighed,
every word measured,
believing that bending
my spine was the only
way to redemption
Assuming that I grew up
with better convictions,
but did I?
Now it's five past midnight,
my mind open wide,
and I promise to love myself
a little more this time
maybe a little more than
anyone else in my sight

There's only so much
I can do tonight.

Unlearn

You will be taught to love and sacrifice.

Selflessness will be glorified,
giving away a part of you,
added as a badge of pride
Pushing you to fathom
building a home in others
painted in colors of victory
But nobody will ever teach you
it's alright to be self-seeking
This time, look out for yourself,
you don't need another soul
to put up a fight

You will be taught to love and sacrifice.

Summer

The summer after you left,
I set myself free.

As I took a deep breath,
the flowers seemed yellower,
the skies seemed brighter,
the wind in my hair gentler,
tangled yet somehow
untangling my soul
I smiled at the silly ways I
could use a chopstick,
and laughed like no one was watching
I took myself out on coffee dates,
and watched my fear of solitude
fade gracefully away
Emptiness in my stomach,
filled with waves of gratitude
The world just seemed better
with my mere existence in it

The summer after you left,
I set myself free.

Conquer

Today I spoke
to the little pockets in my heart.

They said,
I hold fondness for the ones
that needed my love,
warmth for many who
needed to live off my strength,
empathy for souls who never
looked back,
kindness for the ones who
callously left
But,
I found no space for myself in there
So I made a new pocket, step by step
Unapologetically, a little bigger than the rest

Today I spoke
to the little pockets in my heart.

Bloom

When I'm not at my best,
I open my box of flowers.

They remind me often,
despite people who put me down
more often than required,
despite souls that recognize
only their emotions over mine,
I still have some leaves that
want to hold me tenderly
I still have withered petals
who see beauty in my cracks
Best of all,
I have thorns that teach me
every time I bleed,
I will certainly heal

When I'm not at my best,
I open my box of flowers.

Renew

When I wake up tomorrow,
it will be a new beginning,
once again.

Once again as the sun sets
and rises into a new day,
the flowers will still smell this good,
the rays from the sun will still
gently kiss my forehead,
the birds will sound as sweet
as they always do,
the ones who adore me will
still see depth in my soul
The pain within will continue
to nurture my growth
Closed chapters will keep
reminding me of my unseen strength

When I wake up tomorrow,
it will be a new beginning,
once again.

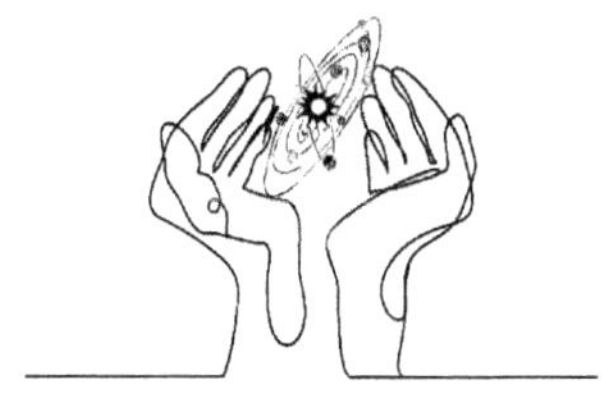

Existence

Here you are and it's
nothing less than magic.

Stardust building in your body,
year after year
Cosmos reshaping for you,
moment after moment
So chaotic yet so well in order,
lifetime after lifetime
Waking up to infinite possibilities,
night after night
And on days that seem hard to get by,
you still reckon your existence as
inconsequential?

Here you are and it's
nothing less than magic.

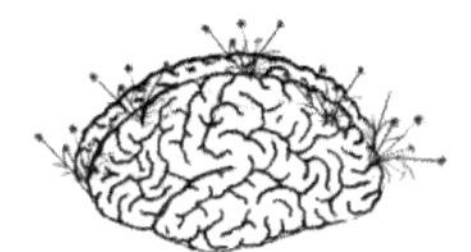

Grace

I hope you choose you.

If they break down your walls
with tenderness and love,
feed you thoughts of being real
with utmost acceptance,
sweep you off your feet with
words nobody else utters,
and whisper holy intentions,
making you crumble in awe,
only to make you believe one day
that you are too much for them,
gracefully take all the love you
hold for yourself and leave

I hope you choose you.

Flow

Just like time,
I wait for none.

Letters written to you
Carefully folded, put away
in my grandmother's powder box,
snuck in the corner of my attic
The scribbles on it have words
that may have slipped through
your careless ways,
but they speak to me of the
warmth that meant a little more
than everything else to me
But I'm glad.
I'm glad that those folded pieces of
paper are mere reminders of
how I have left those moments
gracefully because

Just like time,
I wait for none.

Gratitude

Every time,
I chose love over sin.

I pushed myself towards sanity
as I was told,
shoved those unsolicited
opinions down my throat,
got drenched in tears that
burned my skin,
but decided that hope
is a word I choose to conquer
and not just silently sink in
So here I am with
stories to tell,
no remorse, no regrets,
no bygones I dwell on
Counting everything I have
become by holding some love
for all my tomorrows

But I like to pay a visit
to my sorrows sometimes
Not to crash and crumble,
like my heart once did,
but to remind myself
how beautiful those scars

feel on my bare skin
As I gently leave them where
they effortlessly belong,
I gladly get back to my tomorrows,
with some warmth in knowing that

Every time,
I chose love over sin.